W9-DFH-823

Steadwell Books World Tour
ISRAEL

PRIYA SESHAN
CHRISTOPHER MITTEN

Steadwell Books

Raintree Steck-Vaughn Publishers

A Harcourt Company

Austin · New York
www.raintreesteckvaughn.com

Published by Raintree Steck-Vaughn Publishers,
an imprint of Steck-Vaughn Company

Editor: Simone T. Ribke
Designer: Maria E. Torres

Library of Congress Cataloging-in-Publication Data
Seshan, Sandya.
 Israel / by Sandya and Priya Seshan.
   p. cm. -- (Steadwell books world tour)
 Includes bibliographical references (p.) and index.
 Summary: Describes the country of Israel, including information on its history, geography, government, religions, social life and customs, and some popular tourist sites.
 ISBN 0-7398-5536-0
   1. Israel--Description and travel--Juvenile literature. [1. Israel.] I. Seshan, Priya. II. Series. III. Series

 DS107.5 .S37 2002
 956.94--dc21   2001048964

Printed in the United States of America
10 9 8 7 6 5 4 3 2 1 W 05 04 03 02

Photo acknowledgments
Cover (a) ©Paul A. Souders/CORBIS; cover (b) ©James Davis/CORBIS; cover (c) ©Kevin Cullimore/Getty Images; p.1a ©James Davis/CORBIS; p.1b ©Ted Spiegel/CORBIS; p.1c ©AFP/CORBIS; p.3a ©James Davis/CORBIS; p.3b ©Richard T. Nowitz/CORBIS; p.5a ©Richard T. Nowitz/CORBIS; p.5b ©Harstock; p.6-7 ©Simone Ribke; p.8 ©Hulton Archives/Getty Images; p.13a-b ©Richard T. Nowitz/CORBIS; p.14 ©Simone Ribke; p.15a ©Richard T. Nowitz/CORBIS; p.15b ©Shai Ginott /CORBIS; p.16 ©David H. Wells/CORBIS; p.19 ©Richard T. Nowitz/CORBIS; p.20 ©Simone Ribke; p.21a ©Shai Ginott /CORBIS; p.21b ©Kevin Cullimore/Getty Images; p.23a-b ©Richard T. Nowitz/CORBIS; p.24 ©Alan Puzey/Getty Images; p.25 ©Harvey Lloyd/Getty Images; p.27a ©Richard T. Norwitz/CORBIS; p.27b ©Robert Holmes/CORBIS; p.28 ©Paul A. Souders/CORBIS; p.29a ©Dave Bartruff/CORBIS; p.29b ©AFP/CORBIS; p.30 ©Bryan Peterson/Getty Images; p.31a Gary Braasch /CORBIS; p.31b ©Paul A. Souders/CORBIS; p.33 ©Gary Cralle/Getty Images; p.34 ©FoodPix; p.35 ©Richard T. Nowitz/CORBIS; p.37a ©Paul A. Souders/CORBIS; p.37b ©Stock Food; p.38 ©Paul A. Douders/CORBIS; p.39 ©Paul A. Souders/CORBIS; p.40 ©Reuters/CORBIS; p.41 ©Reuters/CORBIS; p.42 ©David H. Wells/CORBIS; p.43b ©Richard T. Nowitz /CORBIS; p.43c ©Christine Osborne/CORBIS; p.44a ©David Rubinger/TimePix; p.44b ©Hulton Archives/Getty Images; p.44c ©Jacques M. Chenet/CORBIS.

Additional photography by Steck-Vaughn Collection.

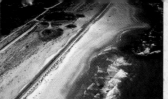

CONTENTS

Welcome to Israel

Shalom! (That means hello in Hebrew!) Would you like to go on a trip to Israel? If you are planning a trip to Israel, this book can help you learn more before you go. But if you are not planning a trip, this book and your imagination can take you there. Get ready to learn about holiday celebrations, interesting people, and fantastic places to visit.

Reader's Tips:

  • *Use the Table of Contents*

In this kind of book, there may be some sections that interest you more than others. Take a look at the page called "Contents." Pick the chapters that interest you and start with those. (Check out the other chapters later.)

  • *Read the Captions*

Don't know what you are looking for? Before you read, flip through the photos in this book. See something you like? Then read the captions next to the photos. The captions will tell you all about what you are looking at. You can always read the text if you want to learn more.

  • *Use the Glossary*

When you see **bold** words in the text, look them up in the Glossary. The Glossary will tell you their meanings. It can be found on page 46.

▲ **ISRAELI CHILDREN IN PURIM COSTUMES**
The celebration of Purim is always fun in Israel.
People dress up in costumes. There are parties
and parades.

▲ **ROMAN RUINS, CAESARIA**
Israel is a great place to experience history firsthand. You
can still see the ruins of many ancient structures, like the
one above.

ISRAEL'S PAST

The State of Israel is one of the youngest countries in the world. It was only formed in 1948! Yet it has some of the world's oldest recorded history. People have lived in Israel for thousands of years. Read on to find out how Israel's past makes Israel what it is today.

Ancient History

Ancient peoples first showed up in Israel 12,000 years ago. About 4,000 years ago, a nation called the Canaanites settled the area. They called it Canaan. In 1800 B.C., the Hebrews arrived. They were the **ancestors** of modern-day Jews. They became known as the Israelites.

In 1020 B.C., the Israelites elected a king named Saul. The kingdom of Israel would last 300 years. Jerusalem was its capital. In 950 B.C., King Solomon built the First Temple there. It was the holiest Jewish site. The Temple was huge and very **ornate**. Kings and queens from neighboring nations came to visit and admire it.

◀ **KING DAVID**
King David ruled Israel around the year 1000 B.C. Too bad no one told this guy. He is dressed up as King David—harp and all! You can see him wandering around Jerusalem's Old City.

▶ **CHURCH OF THE HOLY SEPULCHRE**
This church in Jerusalem is a holy site for Christians. It was built by crusaders in A.D. 1149 on the spot where Jesus was supposedly crucified.

The Diaspora

The Babylonians took over in 586 B.C. They destroyed the Jews' beloved First Temple. Persia allowed the Jews to build the Second Temple in 515 B.C. In 63 B.C., the Roman Empire conquered the area and destroyed the Second Temple. They left behind the temple's Western Wall to remind the Jews of Rome's power. Later, they renamed the entire region Palestine. At this time, Jews began settling all around the world. This is known as the **Diaspora**. Under Roman rule the Christian religion was formed. Israel was the birthplace of its founder, Jesus.

Rome eventually lost control of Palestine. In the 600s, Muslim Arabs conquered the land. Palestine remained mostly Muslim. Around 1100, Christians tried to regain Jerusalem in wars called the Crusades. Meanwhile, the Diaspora continued. Many Jews were **persecuted**, tortured, or hunted. In the late 19th century, the **Zionist** movement was formed. Its goal was to reclaim a Jewish homeland in Palestine—a place

▲ **JERUSALEM RECAPTURED, 1967**
**Israel regained Jerusalem during the Six-Day War in
1967. Above, soldiers stand close to the Wailing Wall.
Since the war, the world has enjoyed free access to this
holy city.**

where the Jews could escape persecution. In World War I,
the British took Palestine from the Ottomans. They made
several promises to the local peoples. One was the Balfour
Declaration. In it, the British promised to establish a
homeland for Jews in Palestine. More than 85,000 Jews
lived there at the time.

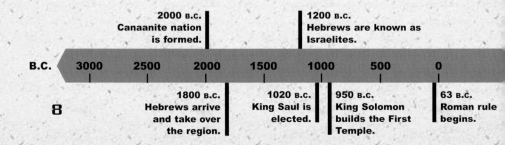

2000 B.C.
Canaanite nation
is formed.

1200 B.C.
Hebrews are known as
Israelites.

B.C. 3000   2500   2000   1500   1000   500   0

1800 B.C.
Hebrews arrive
and take over
the region.

1020 B.C.
King Saul is
elected.

950 B.C.
King Solomon
builds the First
Temple.

63 B.C.
Roman rule
begins.

The Birth of Modern Israel

World War II and the Holocaust changed the world's view on Palestine. Adolf Hitler was the leader of Germany. He was an **anti-Semite**. Part of his political plan for Germany was to kill all the Jews. Over six million Jews were ruthlessly killed across Europe because of Hitler's plan. This horrible time is known as the Holocaust.

Following the war, the United Nations decided the Jews should have a homeland. In 1947, Jews were granted land in Palestine. In 1948, the modern nation of Israel was born.

Modern Israel

Many different nations claimed Palestine as theirs. Arabs in the area were furious. In fact, the Arabs invaded Israel the day after it officially became a nation. The invading countries included neighboring Syria, Egypt, Iraq, and Lebanon. By 1949, the Jews had driven back the invaders against all odds.

Over the next fifty years, Israel would fight several more times with its neighbors. At one point, Arabs who had lived in Israel prior to its independence fled. Israel invited them back. It wanted desperately to live in peace with its Arab neighbors. There has been much violence involved in this cause. Today, Israel continues to work with them on a way to live in peace together. World leaders have become involved in this Middle East peace process. Everyone hopes they will find a solution soon.

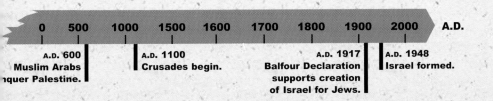

0	500	1000	1500	1600	1700	1800	1900	2000	A.D.

A.D. 600
Muslim Arabs
conquer Palestine.

A.D. 1100
Crusades begin.

A.D. 1917
Balfour Declaration
supports creation
of Israel for Jews.

A.D. 1948
Israel formed.

A LOOK AT ISRAEL'S GEOGRAPHY

Israel is a beautiful country with lots of great scenery. There are gigantic mountains with deep valleys. There are rolling hills with many beautiful plants. There is sprawling desert. There are also long coastlines with deep blue waters. Even though it's a small country, Israel has something for everyone!

Land

Israel is at the point where the continents of Asia, Africa, and Europe meet. The Mediterranean Sea and Egypt border Israel to the west, Syria and Jordan are to the east, and Lebanon is to the north.

In Israel, you will find many different types of land. You can scale mountains or hike through valleys. You can also experience the desert heat. Half of Israel is desert! The Negev Desert is in the south, and it has an area of 4,700 square miles (12,173 sq km). That's pretty huge. So if you go there, make sure to bring your hat and drink plenty of water!

Israel has many mountain ranges. There is the 9,200-foot (2,800 m) high Mount Hermon and the Carmel Mountains in the central region. There is Mount Tabor in the Galilee region. The Jordan River Valley lies in the northeast, near the Sea of Galilee (Lake Kinneret). It has many exotic plants. In the north and central part of Israel are the Mediterranean coastal plains.

► SIZE

Israel is a small country in the Middle East. It is about 300 miles (480 km) long and about 83 miles (135 km) wide. How big is that? Well, look on a map of the United States and locate the state of New Jersey—this will give you a pretty good idea of how big Israel is.

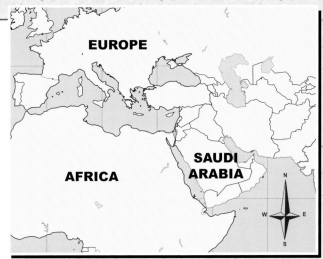

ISRAEL

★ National Capitals
● Major Cities
— Rivers

0 km   50 km   100 km

LEBANON

SYRIA

Safed

Haifa

Deganya

Caesaria

Tel Aviv

Amman

Jerusalem ★

Mediterranean Sea

Gaza

Bethlahem

ISRAEL

JORDAN

Sde Boker

EGYPT

Negev Desert

Eilat

Water

If you like to swim, then Israel is for you! Israel has several bodies of water that are great for swimming. To the west is the Mediterranean Sea. The Mediterranean coastline has lots of beautiful beaches. Tourists and Israelis love to spend time there. The Mediterranean coastline also provides **ports** for boats. One of the most important ports is in the city of Haifa. This is where much of Israel's foreign trade passes through. One of the most fabulous beach towns in this area is Netanya.

The Sea of Galilee, which is also known as the Lake Kinneret, is found in northeast Israel. But perhaps the most important body of water in Israel is the Jordan River. The Jordan is 30 feet (9 m) wide and very shallow. The Jordan River connects with the Lake Kinneret as well as to the Dead Sea. The Dead Sea is in the east. It is the lowest point on Earth—1,312 feet (400 m) below **sea level.**

ISRAEL

★ National Capital
· Major Cities
▲ Mountains
— Rivers

▲ LAKE KINNERET
Also known as the Sea of Galilee, the Kinneret is the lowest freshwater lake in the world. It is 700 feet (213 m) below sea level.

▶ DEAD SEA MUD
This mud is said to cure some illnesses, such as arthritis. It is great for your skin, too. People come from all over to spread this mud on their bodies.

Weather

Israel has a Mediterranean **climate**. It is warm and dry most of the time. The type of weather you experience depends on which part of the country you are in. Northern Israel is usually cooler than southern Israel. Winter is usually rainy and can be chilly, with low temperatures reaching about 40 degrees Fahrenheit (4° C). The summers are long, hot, and dry, so make sure you bring lots of sunscreen—the sun is very strong! There is little rain from June through August. It rains most in northern Israel. Sometimes it rains very hard— up to 5 inches (12.7 cm) of rain can fall in 24 hours! This causes erosion and flooding, which can be a problem. In the desert, there are sometimes **flash floods**!

◄ HOT DESERT
Looking for some adventure? Then head to the Negev Desert. It is a great place to hike. Just be sure to drink plenty of water.

◀ COLD MOUNTAINS
Israel has many different types of weather. Looking to cool off? Head to Mount Hermon in winter. It is a fun place to ski.

▶ THE GOLAN: NOT TOO HOT, NOT TOO COLD
The climate in the north, near the Golan Heights, is quite nice. There are waterfalls, lush hills, and valleys. The best time to visit is spring. Everything is green. All the wildflowers are in bloom.

JERUSALEM: A BIG-CITY SNAPSHOT

▲ THE STREETS OF MODERN JERUSALEM
Above, the Dome of the Rock is visible from the busy streets. It is a holy site to Muslims. It was built in the year A.D. 691.

Jerusalem is over 5,000 years old. Its name means "city of peace." Jews, Muslims, and Christians consider it a holy city.

The Old City

Jerusalem is divided into three parts. These areas are the Old City, East Jerusalem, and West Jerusalem. As you might have guessed, the Old City is the oldest section. Its ancient walls, winding streets, and stone roads will make you feel like you have traveled back in time. Most of the city's religious sites are in this district. Make sure to wear modest clothing (no miniskirts or cut-offs!). This is considered a holy place.

The best way to enter the Old City is through the Jaffa Gate. It is the way that many religious **pilgrims** begin their visit. After entering the Jaffa Gate, head to the Tower of David. This fortress is one of Jerusalem's most impressive buildings. Parts of it were built by the Romans and have survived for nearly two thousand years. There are actually three towers in this fortress. Make sure to climb to the top of at least one of them. The view is great.

Next, check out the Temple Mount. This is where the Jews built the First and Second Temples starting 3,000 years ago. All that remains of the temples today is the Second Temple's Western Wall (or Wailing Wall). This is one of the most important sites in the Jewish religion. Today, two Muslim shrines dominate the Temple Mount—the gold-domed Dome of the Rock and Al-Aqsa Mosque.

West Jerusalem

Jerusalem is also a modern city. After you've toured Jerusalem's ancient buildings, head to West Jerusalem. A good place to start is Kikar Tziyon, or Zion Square. It is West Jerusalem's city center. There is always something interesting happening here. It is near Ben Yehudah Street. This is where you will find cool restaurants and great shopping.

After shopping, visit the Knesset, Israel's parliament. You might see Israeli politicians at work. Then head to the museums. There are two important ones in this district. The first is Yad Va-Shem. This is a museum about the Holocaust and also a **memorial** to those who died in that tragedy. Visiting this museum is a pretty heavy experience. Next, go to the Israel Museum. There you can get a look at the Dead Sea Scrolls. They were found by chance near the Dead Sea. The scrolls are 2,000 years old. They include the oldest known version of the Bible.

East Jerusalem

Start your tour of this district at the Damascus Gate. This is the entrance to the Arab quarter of the Old City. It is a great place to eat falafel and fresh figs.

Next, walk to the Rockefeller Archaeological Museum. Here you will find lots of ancient treasures. Most of the artifacts were found nearby. End your day with a trip to Hebrew University and Mount Scopus. This is the best view of Jerusalem. It is the perfect spot to look over the places you have visited.

▶ THE KNESSET

The Knesset is the Israeli parliament. Out front is a huge menorah (shown on the cover of this book). It is a great spot to snap a few photos.

TOP-10 THINGS TO DO IN JERUSALEM

Having trouble deciding what to do in Jerusalem? Here are 10 things you do not want to miss:

☐ Enter the Old City through the Jaffa Gate.

☐ Climb the Tower of David for a great view of the city.

☐ Visit the Dome of the Rock. (Remember, no cut-offs!)

☐ Head to Ben Yehuda Street for some major shopping.

☐ Learn more about Israeli history at the Israel Museum.

☐ Tour the Knesset and see how Israel's laws are made.

☐ Learn about the Holocaust at Yad Va-Shem.

☐ Eat as much falafel as you can from a street vendor near the Damascus Gate.

☐ Tour the Rockefeller Archaeological Museum.

☐ Watch the sun set from Mount Scopus.

19

Israel has lots of great sights to see. Here are a few that we recommend you start with:

Negev Desert

The Negev Desert is in the southern part of Israel. It makes up more than half of Israel's land. The best time to visit the Negev Desert is from October to May. So what is there to do in this desert? You can hike for miles through its beautiful rock formations. Of course, there are other ways to see the desert besides on foot. You can always go "jeeping"—taking a fast, exciting ride through the sand dunes in a jeep.

While in the Negev, be sure to stop at the Makhtesh Ramon, or the Ramon Crater. It is the world's largest crater. It measures 25 miles (40 km) long and 6 miles (10 km) wide. It is 2,400 feet (732 m) deep! Just make sure you do not fall in.

After checking out the desert, head south to the beaches of Eilat. In Eilat, you can cool down in the clear blue waters of the Red Sea. There is great sea life in its colorful coral reefs. Snorkeling and scuba diving are favorite activities along Eilat's beaches. Make sure to visit the underwater aquarium, too. There are also plenty of restaurants in case you get hungry. The food here is great!

▶ **GOING JEEPING**
The Negev is a popular tourist attraction. Jeeping is one of many exciting things to do—it means taking a fast ride in a jeep through sand dunes.

▼ RAMON CRATER

There is a lot to do at the Ramon Crater. Start at the visitor center. It will tell you all about the history, nature, and geography of the region.

▶ CORAL REEFS, EILAT

The city of Eilat lies at the tip of the Red Sea. Its colorful coral reefs are alive with sea life. Snorkeling is a great way to see exotic fish up close.

Safed

This legendary town lies in the north of Israel near the Lake Kinneret and Mount Meron. Safed is one of the most beautiful spots in the country.

What makes Safed legendary? Almost two thousand years ago a **rabbi** named Shimon Bar-Yochai lived and wrote here. He produced **mystical** texts. These texts have inspired several religious movements within Judaism. After Rabbi Bar-Yochai died, Safed continued to draw great Jewish thinkers. Its golden age, however, came in the 16th century, after the Jews were forced to leave Spain. Many fled to Safed. They set up a new life in this town. They were some of the most important Jewish artists and scholars in the world. The community they built became known as a center of Jewish culture and learning.

Today, Safed enjoys the same reputation. You cannot walk ten steps without bumping into a painter or a sculptor. There are countless art studios and galleries in this town. Be sure to visit some. Maybe you will see something you want to bring home. Maybe you will be inspired to make your own art.

If you visit Safed, make sure to walk along the outskirts. Ancient gravesites surround this beautiful city. Some of the most important Jewish writers and artists are buried here.

◄ COBBLESTONE STREETS
The city of Safed is centuries old. It has narrow, winding cobblestone streets. A walk through this city will make you feel like you have traveled back in time.

▲ MOUNTAINTOP CITY
Safed sits high in the mountains of Northern Galilee. It offers a great view of the Lake Kinneret and the Jordan River.

The Dead Sea and Masada

The Dead Sea is definitely one of Israel's coolest landmarks. Why is it called the Dead Sea? Basically, there is so much salt in the water that absolutely nothing can live in it—so this is not a great place to go fishing. The swimming, however, is lots of fun. All the salt makes things float very easily. There is eight times as much salt as in the ocean. You will float like a cork as you glide along the surface of the water. The other thing you can do on your visit is take a mud bath. Locals say it is one of the healthiest things you can do. Not feeling sick? Take a mud bath anyway! It will be loads of fun.

After your mud bath, take a trip to the nearby hilltop fortress of Masada. Herod the Great built this desert castle in Roman times. It was used to escape the various uprisings in Palestine. Jews who were fighting the Romans later occupied it. However, the Jews living on Masada met a gruesome end. They did not want to be captured by the Romans. So they committed mass suicide within the walls of this ancient fort.

◄ STAYING AFLOAT
Floating in the Dead Sea is fun! The water is so salty that floating is effortless. Just sit back, relax, and enjoy a good read.

▲ ANCIENT RUINS, MASADA
Hiking up this mountain is quite popular. The hike takes hours. Smart hikers start out before sunrise to beat the mid-day heat.

Tel Aviv

People will tell you that Israel is a land of ancient treasures. This is true. But historical sights are not all this country has to offer. Once you've had your fill of museums and monuments, head to Tel Aviv. It has awesome nightlife, great restaurants, and the largest bus station in the world.

To see Tel Aviv at its hippest, head to Dizengoff Street. You can spend all day wandering its shops. You can sip coffee at cafes and watch Israel's coolest people walk by. Just make sure to bring your wallet. Some of these stores can get pretty expensive.

Too much shopping and eating? Head to Jaffa Beach to relax a little. The boardwalk in Jaffa is considered to be a very artsy area. It is a particularly nice place to visit at night. You can sit back, slurp a milkshake, and watch the surf.

When you finish your tour of Tel Aviv, you will want to go to the Central Bus Station. Tel Aviv's bus station is the biggest in the world. Most people in Israel travel by bus. You can get just about anywhere you want to go in Israel from this station. Ready for your next Israeli adventure? Just buy a ticket and hop on board.

▶ **BUS TICKET**
This is a special bus ticket for a one-day trip.

עצמאות בגוש קטיף
כרטיס נסיעה
יום העצמאות תשנ"ה

▼ TEL AVIV SKYLINE

Tel Aviv is crowded and very modern. Many call Tel Aviv "the city that never sleeps." There is always something to see or do.

▶ GETTING AROUND

Most people in Israel use buses to get around. These kids look ready for a day at the beach.

GOING TO SCHOOL IN ISRAEL

Israeli children attend school six days a week. They go to school from ages five to 17. Israeli kids take pretty much the same subjects as you do. They learn and speak in Hebrew, though many schools do teach English as a second language.

After finishing high school, Israelis must serve their country. Usually this means serving in the army. Some Israelis, however, choose to do community service instead. Both the army and community service start at age 18 and last for 20 months. After that, many young people attend college. There are lots of colleges in Israel. Tel Aviv University and Bar Ilan University are two of the better-known schools. There are other colleges in Jerusalem, Haifa, and Tel Aviv as well.

▲ AN ISRAELI CLASSROOM
Classes in Israel are taught in Hebrew. Israeli schoolchildren learn many of the same subjects as you. And sometimes they have to give oral reports, too!

ISRAELI SPORTS

Israelis enjoy a wide variety of sports. Soccer is probably the most popular team sport. Israelis also enjoy hiking, bicycling, camping, and basketball. In the wintertime, Israelis interested in skiing head to Mount Hermon.

One important Israeli sporting event is the Maccabee Games, which are often described as the Israeli Olympics. This event brings together Jewish athletes from all over the world. They compete in just about every event you can think of. Interested in such events as the pole-vault or team handball? Then make sure to put the Maccabee Games on your schedule.

▶ **SHESHBESH**
Sheshbesh is a popular board game in Israel. It is a Middle Eastern form of backgammon. Players roll dice to move their pieces around the board.

◀ **THE MACCABIAH**
The Maccabee Games is an Israeli sporting event much like the Olympics. It is held every four years.

FROM FARMING TO FACTORIES

In Israel, people hold many different types of jobs. They are lawyers, barbers, cooks, and so on. Some businesses produce goods for sale around the world. Israeli factories make things like chemicals, computer products, military equipment, clothing, and fabrics. Israel is also a leader in the world of high-tech electronics. Israelis produce software and the microchips that power computers all over the planet. This country is also famous for one other thing—diamonds. Israeli diamonds are regarded as some of the best in the world. The diamond trade brings in many shekel. The shekel is the kind of money used in Israel.

Many Israelis also work on farms. Israel's farms produce mainly citrus fruits, vegetables, cotton, poultry, and dairy products. Some people live on kibbutzim, which are **communal** farms. On a kibbutz, everyone shares the work and the profits.

Medical research is a popular profession among Israelis. In fact, Israel has the highest percentage of doctors of any country in the world. These doctors are also famous for their breakthrough medical research.

Tourism is another important industry in Israel. The country's warm climate and beautiful beaches make it a great place to visit. So remember, when you are napping in the sand or eating a big Israeli dinner, you are helping Israel's economy.

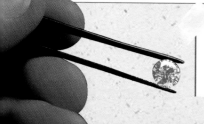

◄ DEALING IN DIAMONDS
Rough, or uncut, diamonds are sent to Israel to be cut and polished. Then they are sold all over the world.

▲ **TOURISM IS BIG BUSINESS**
Souvenir shops sell mostly to tourists.

▲ **FRESH FRUITS AND VEGETABLES**
Israel is famous for its amazing produce. Citrus fruits,
such as these grapefruits, are extra juicy and sweet.

THE ISRAELI GOVERNMENT

Israel is a parliamentary democracy, which means that the leaders are elected. There is a **prime minister** and a president. The prime minister is elected directly by the Israeli people. The president, or nasi, is the head of the state. The nasi serves a term of five years and can be elected only two times. Israelis do not elect the nasi, though. The nasi is elected by the Knesset, which is the **parliament**. The Knesset is made up of 120 people. Knesset members are chosen every four years. Israelis do not directly elect people to the Knesset. Instead, Israelis vote for the political parties they like. The number of votes a party receives determines the number of seats in the Knesset that a party will get.

ISRAEL'S NATIONAL FLAG

A blue Star of David sits in the center of two blue bands on a white background. The Star of David (the Magen David) represents Jewish faith in Israel and is a traditional symbol for the people. The colors of blue and white represent the Tallit, a shawl worn during prayers.

RELIGIONS OF ISRAEL

The State of Israel was founded as a Jewish homeland. The Jewish religion is called Judaism. Followers of Judaism observe the laws of the Torah, the Old Testament of the Bible. More than 80% of Israel's citizens practice Judaism.

Christianity and Islam are the other major religions practiced in Israel. Followers of Christianity are called Christians. They follow the teachings of Jesus found in the New Testament of the Bible. Israel is very holy to Christians because it is where Jesus was born. Followers of Islam are called Muslims. Muslims follow the teachings of a man named Mohammed. These teachings are found in the Book of the Koran. Most of the Arabs who live in Israel are Muslim, but some are also Christian.

▲ HOLY SITES IN JERUSALEM
The Kotel, or Western Wall, is an important Jewish site. This wall is all that remains of the Second Temple, built 2,500 years ago. The Dome of the Rock, seen behind, is an important Muslim site.

ISRAELI FOOD

As many people will tell you, there is nothing quite like Middle Eastern food. Two of the most popular dishes in Israel are falafel and shawarma. Falafel and shawarma shops are found everywhere in Israel. Falafel balls are deep-fried. They are made of ground chickpeas and spices. Shawarma is shavings of lamb or turkey meat that has been slow-roasted on a spit. Shawarma is eaten in pita, much like falafel. Pita bread is flat and round and has a pocket. Israel is also famous for its fabulous produce. You have never tasted anything quite as delicious as fresh Israeli citrus fruits. Israeli vegetables, such as peppers and cucumbers, are sweet and crunchy. Fresh fruits and vegetables play a big part in Israeli cuisine. Many Israelis often eat vegetables at breakfast!

◀ FALAFEL
Falafel is sometimes called the Israeli taco. It is eaten in a pocket of thin pita bread that is stuffed with veggies such as tomatoes and cucumbers—much like a taco.

ISRAELI SALAD

Ingredients:
Large mixing bowl
4 diced tomatoes
1 cucumber, cut into small cubes
1 green pepper, diced
3 tbs lemon juice
2 tbs extra-virgin olive oil
Salt to taste
Black pepper to taste

WARNING:
Never cook or bake by yourself. Always have an adult assist you in the kitchen.

Directions:
Combine all of the above ingredients in the bowl and toss lightly. Chill before serving.

UP CLOSE: THE KIBBUTZIM

A kibbutz is a farm that is run and owned by everyone who lives on it. (The plural is kibbutzim—one kibbutz, many kibbutzim.) The people who live on a kibbutz are considered members. On a kibbutz, everyone shares the work, the responsibilities, and the profits.

Kibbutzim and the Past

Kibbutzim started in the early 1900s. In 1909, the first kibbutz was founded in Daganya, near Lake Kinneret. The first members focused on the importance of the community. They were farmers.

Each kibbutznik, or member, helped raise the children on the kibbutz. Kibbutz children did not live with their parents. Instead, they lived together in a separate children's house. Parents lived in separate houses. Everyone ate dinners together in the common dinner hall. The general idea was that no one person owned anything. Instead, all the members shared ownership. So individuals did not own their own personal TVs or cars. These were shared or kept in the common areas.

At one time, kibbutzim were very popular. In 1990, there were 270 kibbutzim in Israel. At that time it was the largest communal, or community, movement in the world.

▲ **KIBBUTZ DAGANYA**
A kibbutz is a special type of farm found only in Israel.
Daganya was the first kibbutz. It formed in 1909 near
the Lake Kinneret.

FASCINATING FACT

An Israeli that was born and raised in Israel is called a sabra. A sabra is also a popular fruit in Israel. It comes from a cactus. It is very sweet and juicy. But be careful—you will need gloves to remove the spiny peel.

Kibbutzim Today

Today, kibbutzim have changed a lot. Originally they were mostly farmed. However, many kibbutzim today are **industrial**. They may produce plastics, electronics, or clothing.

Children do not live away from their parents anymore. Instead, they live with their parents. Families live in bigger houses. They enjoy owning their own televisions and VCRs. So things are very different than before.

Kibbutzim today face many challenges. The number of kibbutzim is decreasing. There are only 250 kibbutzim in Israel. Two out of three young members leave their kibbutzim to try other things. Only 2% of the Israeli population now lives on kibbutzim.

Kibbutzim are a popular tourist attraction in Israel. Many young tourists go to Israel to work and live on a kibbutz for several months. Kibbutzim welcome such visitors. The kibbutz gives them a place to live and food to eat. Though the future of kibbutzim is unsure, many agree that it is a wonderful and fulfilling way of life.

◀ **KIBBUTZIM AT RISK**
There are fewer people to work on the kibbutzim. Members now hire nonmembers to work so that their kibbutzim can stay in business.

▲ **WORKING ON A KIBBUTZ**
Everyone shares the work on a kibbutz—even visitors. The kibbutz
supplies room and board. In return, visitors work on the kibbutz.

HOLIDAYS

Israel is a Jewish state. Many of Israel's holidays are Jewish religious holidays. Israel also has a number of national holidays. Yom Ha'Atzmaut is Israeli Independence Day. It is celebrated in late April. Yom Ha'Zikaron is the Day of Remembrance. It is dedicated to all the soldiers who fought and died in the Israeli wars.

Israel has a number of other holidays as well. Purim, in March, is a fun holiday. People dress up in costumes. There are parades and parties. Yom Kippur is a very serious Jewish holiday. It usually falls in October. It is a day for fasting and **repentance**. Hanukkah, the Jewish festival of lights, takes place in December. It lasts for eight days. It celebrates the Maccabees' victory over the Greeks in ancient times. Participants light **menorahs**.

Many people who live in Israel are Muslim. One of the most important Muslim holidays is Ramadan. It is a time for personal reflection. During the month of Ramadan, followers will **fast** during the day. At nightfall, they break their fast with a feast.

▲ YOM HA'ATZMAUT: INDEPENDENCE DAY
Above, soldiers take part in Independence Day festivities. Israelis celebrate this day with parades, bonfires, barbecues, and more. Very often, they wear blue and white—the colors of the national flag—to show Israeli pride.

LEARNING THE LANGUAGE

English	Hebrew	How to say it
Peace, hello, goodbye	Shalom	sha-LOME
Excuse me, sorry	S'Licha	slee-HAH
Thank you very much	Toda raba	toe-DAH rah-BAH
Okay	B'Seder	BEH-SAY-dare
Wait!	Regah!	RAY-gah
Good morning	Bokair tov	bow-KARE TOVE
Good evening	Eruv tov	eh-REV TOVE
See you later	L'Hitraot	LEH-HEET-ra-OAT

QUICK FACTS

ISRAEL

Capital ▶
Jerusalem

Borders
Lebanon (N)
Syria (NE)
Jordan (E)
Egypt (SW)
Mediterranean Sea (W)

Area
8,019 square miles
(20,770 sq km)

Population
5,938,093

▼ **Religions Practiced in Israel**

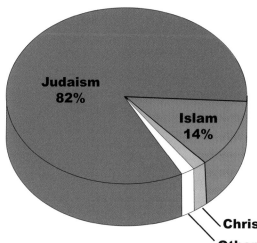

Judaism
82%

Islam
14%

Christianity 2%

Other religions 2%

▼ **Largest Cities**
Jerusalem (567,100 peop
Tel Aviv (355,900)
Haifa (250,000)
Holon (162,800)

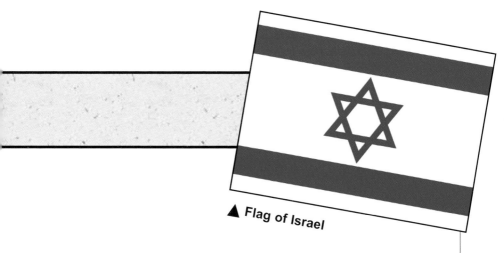

▲ Flag of Israel

Coastline ▶
170 miles (273 km)

Longest River
Jordan River 200 miles
(320 km)

Literacy Rate
92% of all Israeli people
can read

Major Industries
Food processing, diamonds,
textiles, and clothing

Chief Crops
Citrus and other fruits,
vegetables, cotton

Natural Resources
Copper, phosphates, bromide,
potash, clay

◀ **Monetary Unit**
Shekel

PEOPLE TO KNOW

There have been lots of people who have made Israel a great country. Here are just a few:

◀ GOLDA MEIR

Golda Meir was Israel's first female prime minister. She served in the Israeli government for most of her life. However, she did not become prime minister until 1969, when she was 71. Golda Meir died in 1978.

▶ MOSHE DAYAN

Moshe Dayan is one of Israel's true heroes. He led Israeli troops in many of Israel's wars. Dayan was also a skilled leader. He served in several high-level positions in the Israeli government. Dayan was born on a kibbutz in 1915 and died in Tel Aviv in 1981.

◀ ACHINOAM NINI

Achinoam Nini, also known as Noa, is one of Israel's hottest pop stars. Her fame goes far beyond Israel—millions of people around the world enjoy her music.

Want to know more about Israel? Check out the books below.

Burstein, Chaya. *A Kid's Catalog of Israel.* Jewish Publication Society, 1988.
This book tells about the history, culture, stories, and songs of Israel.

Drucker, Malka. *The Family Treasury of Jewish Holidays.* New York: Little, Brown and Co., 1994.
This book gives a history of Jewish holidays and includes recipes, too.

Park, Ted. *Taking Your Camera to Israel.* Austin, TX: Raintree Steck-Vaughn, 2000.
Learn new information about Israel through fascinating full-color photos.

Randall, Ronne. *Food and Festivals: Israel.* Austin, TX: Raintree Steck-Vaughn, 1999.
Discover the tastes and festivals of Israel through this illustrated cookbook.

Silverman, Maida. *Israel: The Founding of a Modern Nation.* New York: Dial Books, 1998.
This book describes the history of Israel from Biblical times to the present.

GLOSSARY

Ancestors (AN-sess-turs)—a person's older relatives who are no longer living

Anti-Semite (AN-tye-SEM-ite)—someone who hates or dislikes Jews

Climate (KLYE-mit)—the weather in a place

Communal (kuh-MYOO-nuhl)—a place that is shared by many people, like a bathroom

Diaspora (dye-AHS-poh-rah)—the resettling of Jews in countries all over the world after exile from Israel

Fast (FAST)—to not eat, usually for a religious reason

Flash floods (FLASH-FLUHDZ)—sudden floods that are caused by heavy rains

Industrial (in-DUSS-tree-uhl)—areas or businesses that have to do with factories and production

Memorial (muh-MOR-ee-uhl)—a special place or way to remember events or people from the past

Menorahs (meh-NO-rah)—special candleholders used in the Jewish religion that hold seven or nine candles

Mystical (MISS-tih-kuhl)—having to do with spiritual beliefs or truth

Ornate (or-NAYT)—highly decorated

Parliament (PAR-luh-muhnt)—an elected group of people who make up the laws in their country

Persecuted (PUR-suh-kyoo-ted)—treated cruelly and unfairly because of having different beliefs

Pilgrims (PIL-gruhmz)—people who travel to a holy place to worship

Ports (PORTS)—areas where ships can safely dock to load and unload cargo

Prime minister (PRIME MIN-uh-ster)—head of state, similar to a president

Rabbi (RAB-eye)—a religious leader for people who are Jewish

Repentance (ri-PEN-tance)—feeling sorry for bad things you have done and promising to change

Sea level (SEE LEV-uhl)—the average level of the ocean's surface, used to measure the height or depth of a place

Zionist (ZYE-uh-nist)—someone who believes that there should be a Jewish homeland in Israel and helps to support it

INDEX